Grab Hold Of Your Miracle

10 Keys to Experiencing Supernatural Miracles

Demontae A. Edmonds

REJOICE
Essential Publishing

Author's website: www.F4Nations.com

Grab Hold Of Your Miracle/Demontae A. Edmonds

ISBN-10: 1-946756-32-6
ISBN-13: 978-1-946756-32-9

Library of Congress Control Number: 2018951471

DEDICATION

This book is dedicated to my wife Jessica Edmonds who has supported and co-labored with me throughout the years in ministry. Also, it is dedicated to the men and women of God who work tirelessly around the world sharing the message of Jesus Christ.

"Jesus lived in the realm of the supernatural and performed unprecedented miracles. He also showed us that nothing happens without faith! In his new book, *Grab Hold of Your Miracle*, Apostle Demontae Edmonds shares amazing Biblical and personal stories of how to live in the supernatural, walk by faith and see the miraculous in your own life!" –

Wendy Griffith
700 Club (Co-Host)
CBN News Watch (News Anchor)

***

I was wondering why you asked me to send you the endorsement. Ole Apostle dropped the ball .Here they go. "This faith inspiring book, *Grab Hold of Your Miracle*, by Apostle Demontae Edmonds is a supernatural handbook for all believers ready to unleash the miraculous power of God through them. This book will empower and activate the personal faith required for Christian believers to access the supernatural in their daily lives. Not only will the reader receive information but tangible impartation on receiving healing breakthroughs and operating in miracles presently just as Jesus did. *Grab Hold of Your Miracle* is power-packed with personal healing testimonies, biblical examples, practical teaching and prophetic revelation on the relevance of miracles today. I highly recommend this book for anyone ready to soar in the matters of the Spirit while simultaneously possessing their own miracles!"

Dr. Hakeem Collins
Champions International
Author of Heaven Declares and Command Your Healing

***

"It has been my privilege and honor to have the Lord Jesus Christ allow my path to cross and connect with such a powerful, anointed, prophetic, apostolic and yet humble vessel of God as Demontae A. Edmonds. *Grab Hold of Your Miracle* is not just a cliche' or gimmick. This book represents the tangible personal testimonies, truths, and affirmations in demonstration by the author, which clearly depicts the miracle working power of God that will literally CHANGE YOUR LIFE!"

Dr. Shirene Anderson-Phillips, Director
IMPACT Global Network
Apostle John Eckhardt, Sr. Pastor/Overseer
Crusaders Church Ministries INT'L.

Contents

FOREWORD...xi

ACKNOWLEDGMENTS.......................xix

INTRODUCTION.....................................1

KEY ONE: Uncommon Faith
                Releases Uncommon
                Miracles...........................3

KEY TWO: Let God Decide
                the "How".......................14

KEY THREE: The Right Place
                at the Right
                Time...............................26

KEY FOUR: Stand on The Word
                of God............................38

KEY FIVE: The Laws of God
                Are Higher.....................50

KEY SIX: Create Your Miracle
                Circle.............................66

KEY SEVEN: Repentance Clears
              the Path..........................77

KEY EIGHT: The Master of
              Miracles..........................86

KEY NINE: Give God Something
              to Work With.................95

KEY TEN: Commit Your Miracle
              to God's Hands 104

ABOUT THE AUTHOR..........................116

Foreword

When I met Demontae Edmond several years ago, I did not yet know him by one of his nicknames today, "The Miracle Man."

Instead, I met this young man with a beautiful wife and family. I observed one thing clearly. What he was busy with-- we used to call "Doin' the Stuff." Rather than just talk about what he might one day do if God helped him, Demontae was working a full-time job while also doing what amounted to full time ministry, literally all over the world. He was "Doin' the stuff" all right!

And while I had not yet published him on the Elijah List, I watched and listened and read the personal prophetic words he gave to me. Even this week, some of those words from years ago, came through exactly as he prophesied them to me regarding the new TV studio he saw.

Yesterday I did research on what he prophesied and I was stunned how accurate they were, even describing the TV Screens at the back of our set—the ones we turned on 3 days ago for a dry run practice. When a young prophetic man (or woman) emerges like this, I try to pay close attention. God had highlighted Demontae to me and He continues to do so today.

So, when I was invited to write the Forward to this book, it just made sense for me to do that. I've been watching and taking notes, both mentally and literally. I've seen only a few years of his early life in ministry and already I'm in awe of what I'm witnessing –I'm stunned at how God is using this young prophet of God.

Pay attention to this man, Demontae Edmonds. He's paid the high cost to arrive at where God has taken him, having obeyed many, if not most of his assignments and tests from God while also repenting when he needed to for missing it with God in how he obeyed. Much of that, you will read about in this book.

As I began to read the manuscript to this book I was struck with an "aha!" moment as I read about Demontae's respect for Dr. Fred Price, who at the end of every broadcast asked his viewers to remember, "We walk by faith and NOT BY SIGHT!"

At this writing, I'm 63 years old- much older than Demontae and yet while only in my mid 20's I would tune into Fred Price's meeting, every Friday night on TBN. Fred Price was my mentor too --albeit on TV only. Dr. Price would repeatedly teach about how "Jesus went about doing good and healing everyone who was oppressed of the devil."

Over and over I heard this teaching until it became clear to me where maladies and sickness all came from. Then I started practicing it. Our first time trying it out, we saw a young woman with a lifetime of arthritis healed in front of us as the Power of God hit her with our simple prayers.

As I ponder this, it turns out there's just one book I wish I would have had way back then around 1981 to help me in my discovery of the Kingdom of God, and miracles, signs and wonders. What book is that? This one, you now hold in your hand, "Grab Hold of Your Miracle!"

There are few who have both the gift of ministry and at the same time have the gift of writing... getting straight to the point, easily conveying to his readers concepts can be very hard to teach in a simple fashion, and yet this author does just that. What a good teacher!

The thing is, as a boy and then a young husband, I had been baptized but I had not yet fallen in love with God nor had I really liked to read the Scriptures.

The Bible was Holy, I knew that. Yes, the Word was about a Big and Holy God but for me and how I was taught back then, God did all those things 2000 years ago and then . . .. well, and HE JUST STOPPED. He had all His miracles codified in the Bible and then it was as if God's job changed to teaching us only how it was "back in the day!" God was sort of telling us there was "nothing new under the sun," or so I thought. I was taught wrong!

One day, acting in faith all that changed in our both our minds, hearts, souls and spirits.

What took my wife and I, now married 40 years...what took us 40 years to discover about God, Demontae Edmonds IS WALKING IN ALL OF IT --NOW!

Yes, years later, I'm now prophesying, praying for the sick, trusting God for huge miracles and seeing them manifest, and watching financial windfalls materialize before our eyes. But what took us four decades to learn, you can grasp the simplest easy-to-understand teaching on all of the above—and just start to obey. You too can do it all NOW.

So no, I didn't get to have this book back in 1981, but the good news is, YOU DO HAVE IT NOW.

But please do me a favor. Do NOT UNDERESTIMATE the power of each key you will learn in this book. They sound so simple, so clear, that you might be tempted to say that things have to sound deeper or more profound to carry the real power and authority to help you do what Demontae is doing. Nothing would be further from the truth.

Read this book. Underline it. Believe what you read. Determine to put these things into practice. Then every year or so, take out this book and look at what you've underlined. Trust me, you'll say, "This stuff really works!"

Steve Shultz
Founder: The Elijah List and ELIJAH STREAMS TV Program

ACKNOWLEDGEMENTS

This book was divinely inspired by the Holy Spirit who has guided us in ministry and allowed us to witness hundreds of supernatural miracles around the world. A special thanks to Donita Gordon who helped me with the writing process and was a great source of inspiration. Thanks to Maurice Wylie who told me it was time to start writing. Thanks to the many family members, pastors, leaders, believers, and business people who have invested in my life and ministry over the years.

Williams family, Edmonds family,Silina Edmonds, Alana Brown, Singelton family, Jordan family, Valerie Briggs-Dorsey, Apostle Sammie Black, Dr. Kim Black, Lisa Pitts, The Twins, Monique Jackson-Ward, Jackie Joyner, Watsons, George Carter, Rena Carter, Dr. Lynderia, Erik Nelson, Richard Peyton, Pastor Chuks, Rev Sally, Tanya S., Wendy , Lashawna Blackburn, Muyiwa, Lola, Nija Means, Steve Means, Jones family, Pastor John L., Michelle, Bill, Prophetess Linda, Mitchell family;

Kyara S. Pastor Maurice, Pastor Hope, Apostle Nigel, Pastor Nikki B, Dr. Yvonne Wright-Dunn, Taylor family (both), McMannen family, Hershell Dunn, Pastor Robbie, Stallings family, Pastor Towanda Walker-Blueitt, Pastor Jack, Pastor Johnny, Pastor Roy O, Aisha, Arlene, Pastor Dale, The entire Freedom 4 the Nations, and many others.

Grab Hold Of Your Miracle

Introduction

Miracles and the supernatural have fascinated mankind since time immemorial. In ancient times, man would often attribute natural phenomenon to "the gods." The advent of science and institutional religion help to do away with the supernatural as being commonly accepted. Today, there is a restoration of faith in God's ability to perform supernatural acts and miraculous deeds on behalf of His children.

The Bible is a book of miracles. From Genesis to Revelation, we read about unusual and unique

1

miracles that God performed to fulfill His plans and purposes in the earth. The very birth of our Lord Jesus Christ was a miracle. His death was followed by a miracle—the resurrection! As believers, we have access to all of the benefits of Kingdom citizenship. This book's practical insights will help to increase your understanding of principles that help to produce miracles or miraculous breakthroughs. Each chapter deals with a specific principle. Your faith will be challenged to Grab Hold of Your Miracle!

Uncommon Faith Releases Uncommon Miracles

"For we walk by faith, not by sight" —2 Corinthians 5:7 (NKJV)

Many Christian households grew up hearing the great Fred Price quote at the end of his broadcast "We walk by faith, not by sight." It is from those simple seven words that we gain an understanding that faith is not seeing with our physical eyes but it is having spiritual vision.

As we begin to explore the principles of accessing the miraculous realm of God, it's important to first examine dimensions of faith. Miracles are directly related to your faith level. Your faith is what grants you the ability to receive from God. One's capacity to receive the gifts of God increases as your faith increases. If there is a desire to experience uncommon miracles, remember miracles are a by-product of raw faith. Faith releases answered prayers but uncommon faith releases the miraculous.

THE CASE OF THE METAL SCREWS

While in a service, God spoke to me, "There is a woman in this meeting that has metal in her lower extremities. Tell the person to come to the altar and I will remove the metal." My mind thought, "Oh boy, this is crazy. What have I just said to this group of people? If anyone comes, they are going to be expecting this miracle!" My mind raced and wondered but faith arose in my heart and I stood on the word that God spoke to me. A woman named Phyllis walked quickly to the altar and said that her feet had metal screws surgically inserted to correct the damage from an earlier automobile accident.

I then heard God say, "Demontae, if you want to see this miracle, then stand on her feet." I looked at her and immediately noted she was probably half my weight and size. In addition, I had on hard bottom men's dress shoes and she had on open toe sandals. I could not afford to miss God! She would be infuriated if I stood on her feet with all of my weight and nothing happened. As soon as I stood on her feet, the power of God struck her like lightning and she was slain in the Spirit.

The next day, she and her husband contacted me and said that she had received a supernatural miracle. That night, there appeared marks on top of her two big toes where the metal screws had been. It was as if an angel of God had supernaturally performed surgery to remove the screws. She could no longer feel the metal because it had miraculously disappeared. God put new bones in the place of where doctors had put metal. What a miracle! This miracle took uncommon faith on my part to obey the voice of God and uncommon faith on her part to respond to the word of the Lord.

To go deeper into the principle of uncommon faith for uncommon miracles, recall the story of Lazarus. The book of John records two sisters by the name of Mary and Martha who called for Jesus because their brother was sick. Once Jesus received word of Lazarus' sickness, He said in John 11:4, "This sickness is not unto death, but for the glory of God, that the Son of God might be glorified." Jesus had such great faith that Lazarus would be miraculously healed that He stayed back where He was for two days before taking action to raise him from the dead. Once Jesus arrived at Lazarus' home, He told Mary and Martha in John 11:40, "Said I not unto thee, that, if thou wouldest believe, thou shouldest see the glory of God? Then Jesus looked up and said, 'Father, I thank you that you have heard me. I knew that you always heard me, but I said this for the benefit of the people standing here, that they may believe that you sent me.' When he had said this, Jesus called in a loud voice, 'Lazarus, come out!' The dead man came out, his hands and feet wrapped with strips of linen, and a cloth around his face." Lazarus was dead four days, and his coming back to life made him a prominent miracle of Jesus' ministry.

FAITH WORKS WHEN YOU WORK IT

God calls the special grace given to individual who perform miracles "The working of miracles" (1 Corinthians 12:10). Without works, you will not see the miraculous power of God. Note the word "working" precedes the term miracles. There must be work or action energized by an uncommon faith that causes God's miracle power to be released. Works give fruit to your faith! Many boast of great faith but are hesitant to take action. Real faith motivates the heart to move and step out of the boat of indifference.

Faith in your heart must be released in the atmosphere by words and actions. "The body without the spirit is dead, so faith without works is dead" (James 2:26). Dead faith results in dead or non-existing works. There comes a time that we have to exercise what we have learned and that which is stored in our hearts. Your works will serve as evidence of your faith.

"You may say thou has faith and I have works, show me thy faith without works and I will show you my faith by my works" —James 2:18.

DESPERATE TIMES CALL FOR DESPERATE MEASURES

2 Kings 4 describes a prophet's widow who was in deep distress. Her husband passed away and it was uncertain if she would remarry. By the complaint of the widow, we understand that she was facing the challenges of being a single parent, living in great debt and feeling helpless. This woman cried out of desperation, saying, "The creditors are coming to take my two sons into slavery." Financial pressure can drain one's mental strength and oppress one emotionally. It is widely known how bank creditors come

to repossess cars and foreclose on homes. When a borrower cannot pay back their loans, it can be stressful but imagine being threatened with a creditor snatching your children. The widowed woman was in a situation of desperation. She needed an uncommon miracle. This woman of God needed supernatural debt cancellation or a major overnight financial breakthrough. Often, uncommon miracles are needed in situations of desperation or life or death circumstances.

In 2 Kings 4:3 (NIV), the prophet Elisha instructed the woman, "Go around and ask all of your neighbors for empty jars." Imagine someone telling a widow who is deeply in debt that the solution to her problem is to borrow again. It would take uncommon faith for her to borrow again while already steeped in debt. Desperate times often call for desperate measures. Her uncommon faith produced an unexpected miracle from her borrowed vessels to inexplicably being filled with oil. The oil continued flowing as long as she had empty vessels to receive it. Imagine having a wallet that no matter how much cash you spend, more cash shows up! Anything is possible with God!

Another example of being in a desperate situation is the woman with the issue of blood in Mark 5:25-34. This woman had an incurable illness and her finances had been drained from seeking medical treatment. The illness was described as having a heavy and unhealthy menstrual cycle. This condition impacted her negatively physically, emotionally, and psychologically. In ancient Hebraic culture, to have an issue of blood or bodily fluids being emitted was to be considered unclean. Individuals afflicted with incurable conditions like blindness, leprosy, etc. were considered to be under a spiritual curse. Some of her challenges would have included not being able to go into public places or socialize with the general population.

Depressed and ostracized, this woman was desperate. Desperation caused her to bypass all of the Levitical ordinances that prohibited a person with bodily emissions from touching others, especially one considered a rabbi like Jesus. In this woman's case, an uncommon desperation produced an uncommon faith. This uncommon faith caused her to press through the crowd and touch the hem of Jesus' garment. Her touch of faith prompted Jesus to respond. Jesus proclaimed, "Who touched me?" There were many touching Him but she touched Him with the touch of uncommon faith and instantly received her miracle. Jesus proclaimed, "Your faith has made you whole."

GET FULL OF THE WORD OF GOD!

There must be a transition from common faith to uncommon faith in order to receive miracle breakthroughs from God. Many have tried to "name it and claim it" but without a revelation of the word of God, it is like driving a car with an empty gas tank. Envision your heart as a gas tank and the word of God as the fuel that goes in it. It's impossible to go far in the Kingdom of God without spiritual fuel. It is the word of God overflowing in a person's heart that does the work to make your faith come alive. Romans 10:17 says, "So then faith cometh by hearing, and hearing by the word of God." Don't just read the Bible but study and meditate upon it until it's digested by your soul.

While attending school, many of us would become anxious when it was time to take finals or mid-term exams. Those who studied and properly prepared for the examinations were less anxious and more confident in their ability to pass the tests. When you become a student of the word of God, life's trials and test may present themselves in your marriage, health, finances, workplace, family and/or life. It is the word of God which is hidden within your heart that will give you the confidence to pass the test. The word will give you the strength like David to overcome whatever obstacle that may come your way. Your faith will move to the uncommon level that will cause you to leap over walls (Psalms 18:29) with God's miraculous power.

"By my God I can leap over a wall"—Psalm 18:29.

Surround yourself with individuals that speak faith and not those that speak doubt and unbelief. Remember faith comes by hearing (Romans 10:17). Doubt and unbelief also can come by hearing when you are exposed to people who are negative and pessimistic. Learn to spend time with those individuals who love to testify about the goodness of God in their lives. Their testimonies will make God more real to you and also encourage you that the same God that blessed them will work miracles on your behalf. Revelation 12:11 states, "We overcome by the Blood of the lamb and the word of our testimony." Don't be afraid to share with others what God has done in your life and you will find that your faith to believe God for greater things will increase.

Let God Decide the "How" for Your Miracle.

YOUR MIRACLE, GOD'S METHOD

You will find in your walk with God that what may seem impossible to man is possible with God. Every circumstance and situation presents a divine opportunity for God to show you **how** He can make a way out of the impossible—"For with God nothing shall be impossible" (Luke 1:37). When we experience God working on our behalf, it increases our faith and builds confidence in God's divine ability.

Prayerfully, after reading this book, you will KNOW for yourself that our God is a God of love and miracles. Miracles often serve as proof of His divine love. Knowing that God is able to do the supernatural is not enough. We must learn to allow God to choose the "how" or the method that every miracle will manifest.

"Trust in the Lord with all thine heart; and lean not unto thine own understanding." —Proverbs 3:5

The lesson in allowing God to decide the manner and method in which a miracle is manifested is something that I learned the hard way. I discovered this principle during a season of personal hardship. In 2006, I was facing serious financial woes and economic oppression. Financial pressure can be one of the greatest challenges that weighs upon a person's mind. It can affect one's emotional state and physical well-being. Just a

few years before I had an income of over six-fig-
ures and within one year, my income decreased
by 70%. Bills fell behind. Way behind! There was
a constant sense of uncertainty about the future
and daily I prayed to God for wisdom to navigate
the affairs of life.

I remember going to a church service and having difficulty lifting my hands to worship or open
my heart to receive the preached message. The
financial strain had left me feeling burned out,
weighed down, and neglected by God. Oftentimes,
we think if we ignore bills, they will go away. Not!
The late notices kept piling up until I had a little stack of them on my kitchen counter. The
collections letters started to show up in colored
envelopes. This is when I knew big trouble was
around the corner.

My options were limited with the help that I
could receive from others because family members had already bailed me out from a previous
financial pitfall. The banks would be of no use
because my once spotless credit score had descended to a poor credit rating. I was between
the proverbial "rock and a hard place."

LET US REASON TOGETHER

My situation went from bad to worse when I received a foreclosure letter in the mail from my mortgage company. They had given me only 60 days to catch up on past due payments or I would lose my home. God blessed me to purchase a single-family home at age 21 and I had no desire to be homeless. This all transpired during the winter months. I lived in an older home where the monthly heating bill was excessive. Already I had received notices from the local electric company stating that I had 30 days to pay the past due amount or my lights would be turned off.

In duress, I went upstairs in my house, fell on my knees, and pleaded with God to deliver me and send a miracle. In prayer, I talk to my heavenly Father as if He was my natural father. I began to reason with God that He was the one that initially blessed me with a great financial miracle to purchase a home at such a young age. I reminded God how I had been faithful with praying and reading my Bible daily. After all, it would be a great embarrassment for me to be kicked out of my house!

"Come let us reason together!" —Isaiah 1:18

I pleaded my case and reasoned with God according to Scripture. Daily, I would remind God of His promises and pray for a major financial miracle. Each day, I would hope for a phone call or visit from someone with the announcement that God had spoken to them to give me a lump sum of money. It didn't happen the way I had envisioned. I no longer felt like I was between a rock and a hard place. I felt like I was under the rock and needed God to lift it off of my head. There is an old saying, "When you can't stand the heat, get out of the kitchen." I would like to share my own saying, "when you can't stand the heat, pray and then pray some more!" The Bible says in James 5:16, "The effectual fervent prayer of a righteous man availeth much." Praying with fervency means to pray with passion or to pray with fire! I began to turn up the heat with my prayer time.

One day, some friends invited me over to their home. This particular couple was worth millions of dollars. They would often entertain me at their home and invite me over for dinner. After dinner, I rode with the husband back to my house and he began to question me about my financial situation. While driving, I began to sing "THIS IS YOUR MIRACLE!" within my head. I'm riding with a multi-millionaire and he is asking me about my money situation and present condition in life. A big check that would solve all of my monetary woes was just around the corner. In a matter of minutes, I would be leaping for joy and praising God for the financial miracle. Sadly, the night did not end the way I had hoped. He made inquiry about my finances but he offered no assistance. Honestly, I felt somewhat offended and confused. My faith felt like a balloon that had just been instantly popped. That night, I went to pray but felt so defeated that it was difficult to get any words out of my mouth to God.

The next day, I decided to pray but not mention my predicament to God. I just wanted to enjoy reading the Word of God and have my intimate time of prayer. Sometimes we can focus so much on our problems that we forget to enjoy the personal time with God. When I finished singing and praying to God, I left my time of devotion with a sense of peace. Momentary peace is better than no peace at all. Besides, in just a few weeks, I would be facing a power outage and foreclosure.

One morning, I felt prompted to log into my mortgage account online and just face the music. I was avoiding looking into my account because I knew it was three months past due and I really didn't have any money to pay the balance down. When I logged on and looked at the amount owed, it said $0. My mind began to race and I felt maybe I was reviewing the wrong information on the account details page. A second glance revealed that my first view was correct. The balance owed was zero. As I checked the payments tab on the account, it showed that somehow someway the total amount owed on the delinquent mortgage amount had been paid.

I knew that I didn't pay it because I didn't have the money. My family members couldn't have paid it because I had purposely withheld them from my plight. They had already bailed me out of a previous situation and no one knew the financial trouble I was in. It was a God-given miracle! All the while, I was waiting for God to send someone to give me money to pay the bill, but He had already caused the bill to be paid without the money ever touching my hands. I felt God was ignoring my prayers but He had already showed out on my behalf.

There was a sigh of relief as one of my two major financial problems had been taken care of with an untraceable miracle. The second problem of the electric bill being months behind continued to be a threat. At least, sitting in a dark house was better than being kicked out of a foreclosed one. About a week later, my electric bill arrived in the mail. The previous bill had a past due balance close to $1000. I slowly opened the bill and to my surprise, it was a $600 balance. God immediately had me to remember the mortgage miracle from the week before. He had favored me once again by lowering the electricity bill. As I paid a small amount on the bill, I prayed that God would not allow my electricity to be disconnected.

The next month, the bill arrived again and this time, it said I only owed $300. Each month, to my unbelief, the bill would decrease without me making the minimum payment. Finally, for four months, the bill reported that the electric company owed me money! Experiencing this financial breakthrough caused me to worship and praise God for having mercy upon me. God performed a miracle and the electricity bill was supernaturally paid! Just like the miracle before He chose HOW it would happen. No one gave me money directly and I didn't have to spend my own money. God chose "HOW" the miracle would manifest in both of these predicaments.

NAAMAN HEALED OF LEPROSY

We have to be cautious not to allow our personal experiences to become doctrine. I am a firm believer that the same principles I teach should also be found and rooted in the Word of God. The Bible is an infallible source of revelation about God and His Kingdom. A great example of why it's important to let God decide "how" for your miracle is in a story with the prophet Elisha and Naaman. In 2 Kings 5, we read about Naaman the

Syrian — "He was a great man with his master, and honorable, because by him God had given deliverance to the Syrians. He was a mighty man of valor but he was a leper."

Naaman may be viewed as a General Patton or Julius Caesar of his day. He had respect, honor, favor, and prestige but he was a leper. Leprosy is a contagious disease that affects a person's nerves, muscles, and skin causing discoloration, pain, and in severe cases deformity. Often in ancient times, one afflicted with leprosy was considered under a curse or divine judgment from the "gods." Everyone that he came into contact with him would automatically see and know that he was infected. In fear for their own safety, many would have ostracized or avoided him.

I believe that Naaman would have traded all of his successes and accolades in exchange for being healed of this terrible disease. Due to the fact that leprosy is an incurable disease, Naaman needed a supernatural miracle that only heaven could supply. Words got back to General Naaman that there was a prophet of God that could cure him. I'm sure Naaman was skeptical but also desperate for healing. He had the King of Syria send a letter to the King of Israel making an official request for Elisha the prophet to heal the great General. This task was so great that the King of Israel became afraid and began to cry out to God. Word reached Elisha about the situation and he accepted the spiritual challenge to prove to the Syrians that the God of Israel was the one true God of miracles.

Naaman appeared before Elisha with his horses and chariot and stood at the door seeking his miracle. He expected the great prophet to come out of his house and do some great religious ceremony full of pomp and showmanship before calling on God to heal him. Many religions of the day involved elaborate ceremonies to invoke the presence of their false gods.

Elisha did not even come out of his house but sent his servant to tell Naaman, "Go and wash in the Jordan seven times and then your flesh will be made clean." Naaman, offended at the method that Elisha suggested for his miracle, questioned Elisha's prophetic integrity. Naaman said, "Behold, I thought, He would surely come out to me, and stand, and call on the name of the

Lord his God, and strike his hand over the place, and cure me of my leprosy." He thought he could choose the "how" by which the miracle would be performed. It is God who chooses the method of each miracle. Verse 13 says, "And his servants came near, and spake unto him, and said, My father, if the prophet had bid thee do some great thing, wouldest thou not have done it? how much rather then, when he saith to thee, Wash, and be clean?" Naaman's servant talked sense to him and convinced him to follow the prophet's instructions. He was made whole just as God promised through His servant. He believed for a miracle and received it but God dictated the method of delivery.

The Right Place at the Right Time

"LOCATION! LOCATION! LOCATION!"

"Location! Location! Location!" is a mantra familiar to real estate investors. In the 1970s and 1980s, real estate investors would use this phrase to stress the importance of a geographical location when purchasing property. It was believed that a property's location was just as important as the property itself. Big development firms would target highly prized and trafficked areas that they felt would appreciate in value due to the location. In the Kingdom of God, at times, it is highly important to be at the right place at the right time.

The Kingdom of God exists anywhere that faith in Jesus Christ is present and the Holy Spirit is in operation. Many of Christ's followers were waiting for a return of the rulership of King David and a militant takeover by a new Messiah who would overthrow the Roman government. Jesus had to explain to His disciples that while they were waiting for a physical kingdom to manifest, the Kingdom of God was already in their midst.

"Repent for the Kingdom of God is at hand" —
Matthew 3:2

There was no longer a need to wait for the promise of a material kingdom. Although the Kingdom of God was invisible, it was nevertheless present. Many were expecting a physical Judaic kingdom that would overthrow Roman rule. In contrast, Jesus taught His disciples how to access the invisible Kingdom of heaven. God is omnipresent, which means He is everywhere. Therefore, His Kingdom is an omnipresent Kingdom with special times in which the work of the Holy Spirit takes on heightened action.

TROUBLED WATERS

John 5:1-4 says, "Now there is at Jerusalem by the sheep market a pool, which is called in the Hebrew tongue Bethesda, having five porches. In these lay a great multitude of impotent folk, of blind, halt, withered, waiting for the moving of the water. An angel went down at a certain season into the pool and troubled the water: whosoever then first after the troubling of the water stepped in was made whole of whatsoever disease he had."

What an unusual phenomenon! Take a moment and picture this in your mind. This was a pool where sick and physically challenged people gathered for the one purpose to be healed. They knew that at a certain time, an angel would manifest and stir up the waters and whoever stepped in was made whole. Could you imagine it? If the Pool of Bethesda existed in modern times, it would have been worthy of an episode on the television show *Unsolved Mysteries*. Picture all of the people who were crippled, plagued, in pain, and with diseases fighting and pushing each other to be the first to get into the healing waters.

There were many blind, deaf, sick, demonized, and lepers in Israel in the days of Jesus' ministry. They all could have traveled and been healed at this miracle pool. During the lifetime of Jesus, we only have a record of people being healed under His ministry, the disciples, and the Pool of Bethesda. Those that were at the right place at the right time would be healed. Location! Location! Location!

TIMING IS EVERYTHING

John 5:4 says the angel went down at a "certain season." Those in need of a miracle would have to grab hold of not only being at the right place but being there at the right time. Man may be subjected to either kairos or chronological time. Merriam-Webster Dictionary defines chronological time this way: "of, or related or arranged in or according to the order of time." When one operates under chronological time, things happen in natural sequential order; and life is predictable. Life may seem mundane and routine. Rarely do miracles happen when we walk according to the chronological time scale.

In contrast, there exists kairos time and the kairos moment. Merriam-Webster Dictionary defines kairos as, "a time when conditions are right for the accomplishment of a crucial action, the decisive and opportune moment." The kairos moment is a divine opening for miracles and supernatural breakthroughs to happen. It is an open window for God to do what man says is impossible. As you release your faith, you begin to step from under the influence of chronological time into the window of the kairos moment. Suddenly, a window opens for you to grab hold of your miracle. This is when you are not only at the right place but you have tapped into the right time!

The prophet Daniel, who was also a political leader in the empires of Babylon and Persia, experienced a kairos encounter. Daniel 10:2 states, "Daniel was mourning three full weeks." Daniel was grieved about the captivity of the children of Israel and how they were subjugated to Babylonian rule. He prayed three full weeks for the restoration of the nation of Israel. For twenty days, he encountered discouragement and uncertainty. Often when praying, we struggle with believing that God will answer us and with the timing of our prayers being answered.

On the 21st day, Daniel experienced the kairos moment. The window opened when an angel of God visited him with revelation in response to his prayers. Talk about a miracle. Three weeks of silence, then an angel showed up. Many pray and seek God for a breakthrough but quit right before the kairos moment appears with answers to their prayers.

A NEW BODY PART

One day, while in prayer, it came into my heart to call a dear sister named Valerie and tell her, "God says if you come to the church service this Friday night, He will heal you and give you a new kidney!" She trusted me as a man of God, but doubt still crept in. This was an outrageous promise to someone who had been diagnosed by a medical specialist with needing surgery or a potential kidney replacement. Her natural mind got the best of her and she decided to drive to the hospital's emergency room but somehow ended up in our church's parking lot. God wanted her at the right place at the right time for the right miracle.

During the service, God had me lay hands on her and decree a new miracle kidney. Two weeks later, Valerie returned to testify and share the good news of the miracle that she had received. Her doctors were astonished upon examination to find all of the issues with her kidney had mysteriously disappeared. They said, "It looks like you have a brand-new kidney!" Only Jesus could work a miracle of this measure!

It pays to be at the right place, at the right time. Many times, we pray for a miracle or break-through and when God says, "Get up and go", we fail to take action. Often your miracle won't drop right into your lap but will require you to move when God is moving. It also requires you to move to where God is moving! Jesus told the people of His day, "There were many lepers in the days of Elisha the prophet but none of them were healed except Naaman the Syrian." Naaman was willing to step out on faith, leave his comfort zone, and go to a rival nation in order to be positioned to receive a miracle from God! Ask God to position you for a miracle!

DON'T LEAVE THE PLACE CALLED THERE

I remember once God told me to call a special service named "Night of Divine Healing." It was only the second time that God had our ministry advertise in advance that people would be healed and delivered. I peeked from behind the back room into the sanctuary to see the room filled with believers ready to see what God would do. Many were spectators who had come unsure if God would show up with His healing power. A small degree of anxiety hit me and I quickly disappeared into a private place to pray one more time and seek the face of God. I asked God to manifest His presence and prove that Jesus was still alive to those who were present. Suddenly, I felt a surge of electricity all over my body. This was a reassurance from the Spirit of God that He was with me and about to set many captives free.

While in prayer, I heard the Lord say, "Pray for those suffering from paralysis and seizures and I will heal them." I kept these words in my heart as I emerged from the back room to join in during the time of worship and preached the Word to the attendees. When it was time for altar ministry, boldly I proclaimed, "God is about to heal those suffering from strokes and paralysis." Several came up for prayer and were immediately slain by the power of God. Although several testified that they felt immediate relief and mobility restored to them, in my spirit, I felt as if God did not receive the full glory that He desired from the moment.

After the meeting, one of our church members informed me that a certain local pastor had attended the meeting with his son. This pastor was respected and oversaw a larger-sized ministry. I did not recall seeing the pastor at the meeting but he came in with his son who had physical shakes and trembles. He sat around anxiously for ten minutes before the meeting but seemed to have gotten nervous and left. I knew by the Spirit of God that this pastor had brought his son who was suffering from a major condition to be healed but got out of position because he felt uncomfortable in an unfamiliar place.

THE PLACE FOR NEW

God does new and unfamiliar things to us when we simply "get up and go!" Our resolve to "get up and go" tells God that we are open to change. In going, we demonstrate our trust in God's voice. In going, we show our desire for change. One woman of God shared with me once that God spoke to her by saying, "To stay is to remain." Merriam-Webster dictionary defines *remain* as "to continue unchanged." Many of us have felt that we are just going through the routine of life and fallen into a pit of mundane living. Our God is a God of movement and action. Note that living or experiencing life is related to movement. We must be reminded of James 2:26, "Faith without works is dead." In going, we give feet to our faith.

"For in him we live, and move, and have our being"
—Acts 17:28

Jesus would often rise before day and go to a solitary place where He would pray. Many of the disciples who followed Him would seek after Him from town to town. The disciples had just experienced a major revival in the town of Capernaum. The city-goers there desired more of His ministry and placed a great demand upon His presence. Instead of staying put in that town and relying on His previous success, Jesus began to pray. As He prayed, God spoke to Him to go to the next town. Christ exclaimed in John 10:10, *"...I have come that they might have life and life more abundantly."* Jesus consistently lived in the realm of supernatural and unprecedented miracles. If we study His life, we see that Jesus was constantly on the go under the unction of the Holy Spirit. He knew that He needed to be at the right place at the right time to stay in God's supernatural flow.

Stand On the Word of God

THERE IS NO PLACE LIKE HOME

In 2002, I was close to finishing college and living with relatives. My aunt and uncle had been gracious to allow me to stay at their home while pursuing a college degree. While in school, I worked a part-time job to support my school expenses and livelihood. It came into my heart to purchase my own home after graduating from college.

The usual process for a young person is to first rent an apartment. After years of saving money, building one's credit score, and adjusting to independent living, typically one would buy their first home. After reading an article in a magazine, I discovered the benefits of being a home owner. Home owners receive tax deductions, lower monthly payments, greater privacy, equity, and independence from a landlord. This same article discussed the disadvantages of being a renter. I believed that God used this reading material to stir up in my heart a desire not to rent but to purchase my own home at age 21.

My desire for a house had increased each day after first reading the magazine article. Answers to prayer do not begin with the words spoken out into the physical realm but with the desire expressed from the soul of man.

"Whatsoever you desire, when you pray, believe that you receive them"—(Mark 11:24).

We often fail to recognize that there are pre-requisites for having a successful prayer. We must have a heart's desire in order to see what we are praying for come to pass. Praying without a true desire to receive what we are asking for is likened unto speaking empty words that fall on deaf ears. This principle is seen within the story of the angel that visited the prophet Daniel. "Then he said unto me; fear not Daniel; for from the first day that thou set thine heart to understand and chasten thyself before thy God, thy words were heard, and I have come for thy words" (Daniel 10:12). It didn't take heaven weeks to initiate a response to Daniel's prayers, but his great desire for the liberation of the children of Israel captured heaven's attention.

GIVE AND IT SHALL BE GIVEN

One afternoon, I prayed beside my bed asking God to bless me with money to buy my own house. Also, I had a vehicle that was costing me a lot of money to constantly repair. It now had an issue with its catalytic converter and both oxygen sensors. Having a heart full of faith caused me to ask God for resources for both a new vehicle and a new home. I began to give God several reasons why it was beneficial for me to own and not rent. Also, I pleaded with Him that as a tither, I expected Him to open the windows of heaven on my behalf (Malachi 3:10).

While praying, a small voice interrupted my request to God for money. "Give $1100 to the Inspiration Television Network." I jumped off of my knees and said, "Who said that?" I immediately thought it was the enemy and said, "Devil, I bind you from hindering my prayer time."

As a young believer, I had only heard the voice of God clearly a few times and it was difficult to distinguish if it was God's voice or another. I went back into prayer asking God again for a certain amount to put down as a deposit on a house and a new car. Again, the same small voice said to me, "Sow $1100 to Inspiration Television Network." I left from praying and said to myself, "This must be my own mind playing tricks with me!" Upon returning to prayer, I shared with God how I was not trying to give away money. I was the one in

need of money! The same voice spoke a third time
the exact same words.

Upon discerning that this voice was indeed the
voice of God, my natural mind kicked in. "Where
would I get $1100?" I only had $300 in my bank
account. I replied to God, "God, if that is truly you
speaking, then you must know that I do not have
$1100." In an instant, God gave me a strategy
on how to obtain the money. He said in the same
voice and tone, "Go and borrow money from your
bank." I didn't have any credit cards, never borrowed from a bank, and possessed no credit history. I was doubtful that the credit union which
I banked with would lend me money with such a
lack of financial history. To my surprise, I was instantly approved for a $1500 loan after complet-
ing a ten-minute online application. That same
day, I obeyed the voice of God and sent a check
to the Inspiration Television Network for $1100.

Anticipation of a supernatural miracle filled
my heart for the days and weeks which followed.
There was a newly found confidence because
I knew that I heard the voice of God. More im-
portantly, I knew that I obeyed the voice of God.

Daily, my faith was being enlarged as I would read from the word of God. Certain scriptures such as Luke 6:38 and 2 Corinthians 9:6 circulated within my mind.

"Give and it shall be given unto you" —Luke 6:38.

I stood on 2 Corinthians 9:6, *"He who sows generously will also reap generously."* In my mind, a supernatural financial breakthrough was just around the corner. I began to confess the Word of God daily and believed that God was going to bless me with at least $30,000. A decree of $30,000 was made because Matthew 13:8 speaks of the sower who sowed seed that fell upon "good ground" and "brought forth fruit, some a hundred-fold, some sixty-fold, and some thirty-fold." I knew that God chose the ground for me to sow into and it was good ground. Secondly, my faith was strong enough to multiply the seed sown. The $1100 x 30 would be over $30,000. Matthew 13:8 doesn't necessarily mean that if you give $100, you will receive $3000, $6000, or $10,000. As a young believer, I took this scripture at face value. The scripture reveals how our faith level and environment can affect the yield we receive on seeds sown.

God honored my sacrificial seed and act of obedience. Within a few months, I received a $10,000 check from my job for being the employee of the year at my local job site. In addition, I was the top performer for the organization in my entire division that operated branch offices in three different states. For this accomplishment, I was blessed with a $50,000 check. $60,000 in addition to my regular income was my sixty-fold return on the $1100 miracle seed! In a few months, God's favor did more for me financially than I could have done out of my own ability in two or three years.

GREAT EXPECTATIONS

Daily, I expected a miracle harvest. I would check the mailbox multiple times. Mail delivery would arrive each day between noon and 1:00 pm. I would check the mail at this time but also run out to the mailbox late in the day. My miracle was around the corner. I remember my aunt teasing me saying, "Why do you go to the mailbox multiple times every day? No money is going to show up for you in the mail." I followed the admonition of Reverend Jesse Jackson and, "kept hope alive." I wasn't sure how my miracle would manifest, but I was absolutely convinced that it would happen.

As believers, we must understand that miracles don't just instantly happen. There is always a process involved before a miracle manifests. The miracle may seem instant and supernatural. One must realize there are often hidden, unknown, and unseen variables involved in the production of the miraculous. One of the principles that I have found vital in activating the spiritual force of the Kingdom of God to produce a miracle is found in 1 Corinthians 3:6. The Apostle Paul writes to the church of Corinthians and tells them, "I have planted. Apollos watered; but God gave the increase." An examination of this scripture reveals increase doesn't happen by chance.

Many pray for increase, breakthrough, or deliverance but neglect the prerequisites of planting and watering. Miracles happen when we plant and sow on both the spiritual plane and in the natural realm. Often time preachers instruct their congregants to tithe and sow financial offerings while expecting a harvest. The issue with this is that only one half of Paul's formula for increase is being utilized. Money seed is sown on the material plane, but there must be corresponding sowing in the realm of the Spirit.

What can one sow into the realm of the Spirit? One can sow the right attitude and faith when giving! Every action gives off an energy that is deposited into the spiritual realm. Energies that are counterproductive to the miraculous are doubt, unbelief, bitterness, stinginess, and unforgiveness. Some energies that are productive for the miraculous are faith, joy, love, and kindness. That is one of the reasons that 2 Corinthians 9:7 says, "God loves a cheerful giver." God doesn't just want our money. He desires the love attached to the money or seed sown. The supernatural shows up when we are serving God not out of compulsion, fear, or legalism but out of a heart filled with a great love for God.

SPEAK YOUR MIRACLE

Jesus shares in Mark 4:14 that, "The sower sows the word!" One of the foundational principles I learned is that many neglect to sow the word of God when seeking a miracle. Miracles often appear sudden, instant, and supernatural, but there is always a hidden process involved. All miracles begin with the Word of God being released into the ethereal atmosphere. We see this principle in operation when reading Genesis 1. God the creator of all the universe demonstrates the power of the spoken word. His word is what initiated the creative supernatural process.

"In the beginning God created the heavens and the earth. And the earth was void and without form, and void; and darkness was upon the face of the deep. And the Spirit of God moved upon the face of waters. And God said let there be light; and there was light. And God saw the light, that it was good" —Genesis 1:1-4.

Pay close attention to the fact that before God "saw," He first "spoke." Speak and stand on the word of God and then see the manifestation of your faith. Note the earth was empty, undeveloped, and formless. The power of the spoken word brought order where there was previously chaos, form where there was formlessness, and light where there had been darkness. God spoke into creation before He created man to work the land and govern the earth. Many times, we try to use our natural ability, physical labor, and intellect to solve issues and overcome problems without first speaking the Word. When the Word of God is spoken, you become the sower of the word.

A good farmer knows that before he can expect a harvest, he must first sow his seed. Too often, we take our own actions without following God's written Word for direction. When not experiencing positive results, one may become frustrated and begin to lose confidence in the word of God. Instead, we must recondition our thinking to seek and speak the Word of God. When the Word of God is spoken, it goes out ahead of us to bring its own self into reality in our life. God says in Isaiah 45:2, "I will go before thee and make the crooked places straight." When God's Word goes ahead of us, God Himself backs His word to make sure it accomplishes what is purposed to do (Isaiah 55:11).

Speak, sow, and stand on the Word of God. One can stand on the Word of God when you know you have spoken and acted in faith. The written Word (Logos) turns into the living word (rhema) when it is spoken and acted upon (sowed) in faith. The Apostle Paul says in 2 Corinthians 4:13, "We having the same spirit of faith, as it is written, I believed, and there I have spoken. We also believe and therefore speak." A heart full of faith is a heart posed to receive supernatural miracles from God. A heart full of faith can speak the Word and stand strong believing what has been spoken will come to pass. A heart full of faith can act on the Word and stand strong knowing that the act of faith will produce results. Standing in faith waiting and trusting for God to release a miracle is often the toughest part of the supernatural process. Standing without waiver displays confidence in God and His Word.

" Having done all, to stand" —Ephesians 6:13.

The Laws of God Are Higher Than the Laws of Man

THE FLOATING AXE HEAD

One of my favorite stories in the Bible is found in 2 Kings Chapter 6. In this chapter, we see a different aspect of Prophet Elisha's ministration. Often in scripture, we witness the prophets praying, prophesying, decreeing judgments, and working miracles. In this chapter, the understudies of Elisha presented him with a housing dilemma. The structure where they lived together had become too small and crowded for them. Although Elisha operated in great prophetic insight and supernatural power, there were still tasks that required old-fashioned sweat and labor. They all agreed to build a new house that would accommodate what appeared to serve the dual purposes of being living quarters and school of ministry.

In verse 5, one of the young men cried out as the axe head of the instrument that he was using to cut down wood flew into the water. The river Jordan was a nearby forest where timber could be cut down to build their new structure. 2 Kings 6:5 says, "But as one was felling a beam, the axe head fell into the water; and he cried, and said, Alas my master it was borrowed!" In modern times, if we lose an axe or axe head, we could just go to our local hardware store and purchase another for a low price. In ancient times, if you were to lose a sword, axe head, or any metal object, it was much more difficult to replace as metal was harder to obtain; and during certain periods in Israel's history, metal was scarce. Compounding this young man's problem was the fact that the axe head was borrowed. Not only would there exist a need to replace the axe head to be able to cut down wood to build the new house, he would also need to repay the person that loaned it to him.

The young pupil presented his dilemma to his master Elisha. Elisha, ever ready for a challenge, stepped out on faith and was used by God to work a miracle. 2 Kings 6:6 says, "And the man of God said, Where fell it? and he showed him the place. And he cut down a stick, and cast it in thither; and the iron did swim!" The axe head was retrieved through a supernatural act by the prophet. They both faced the same dilemma of the sunken axe head but took two different courses of action. The young man cried out of fear. Elisha acted out of faith.

As we dissect this miracle, we must examine the mindset of the young man juxtaposed to the mindset of the seasoned Prophet Elisha. The young man minded the laws of man. The physical science laws of buoyancy say objects with a high density (molecules packed tightly together) sink in water. An axe head would have been made of some type of dense metal strong enough to cut wood. Elisha ignored the laws of man—nature— and looked to the laws of God. He knew that that the law of faith could override even the natural elements and principles of physical science.

When we focus on the laws and limitations of men, we become like the axe head when it began to sink. But when we allow the laws of God to rule in our hearts, we become like the swimming axe head buoyantly lifted above every situation. Elisha performed the miracle causing the axe head to ride to the surface by throwing a stick into the water. In the natural, it does not seem like a small stick would do any good to retrieve the axe head. He would have been better to use a rope and net to try to fish for the axe head. We read that he threw the stick into the Jordan River, but do you know what he really threw into the water? He threw his faith and awareness of God into the water!

In Acts 19:11-12, scriptures say, "God worked
special miracles through hands of Paul. And so
that from his body were brought unto the sick
handkerchiefs or aprons, and the diseases departed from them, and the evil spirits went out
of them." Napkins and aprons are like the little
stick, as they have no special magical or divine
powers within themselves; but when endued with
faith and the Spirit of God, they became endowed
with the miracle-working power. They simply
served as points of contact for both Elisha and
Paul to release their faith that the power of God
would overcome the laws of man.

CASE OF THE RECOVERED CAR

I awoke one morning to the eerie feeling that
today was going to be different but not in a good
way. I looked outside my living room window
only to discover that my black Toyota Camry was
missing. Immediately, I began to panic. My first
thought was that someone had stolen my car. It
was a brand-new car with dark tints and shiny
chrome rims that would have been appealing to
car thieves. I called the local police department
to report the missing vehicle and they informed

me that the car was not stolen but that it had been repossessed by the creditor. My heart sank and mixed emotions began to flood my soul. I felt violated, embarrassed, upset, sad, and baffled all at once.

After collecting myself and steadying my emotions, I began to plot out a course of action to retrieve the vehicle back. I called the tow company and they said they were powerless to help me. The decision had to be made by the creditor that was the auto financing company. I called the creditor and they refused to offer me any type of payment arrangements or negotiations. One of my good friends was a great haggler, negotiator, and business person. I enlisted her to call the creditor on my behalf and use her skill sets to coerce the company to return my car if I paid all arrears and a future payment. Even her actions were stonewalled. The finance company was adamant that it was company policy not to return any repossessed vehicles.

Disappointment began to turn into despair. I opened my Bible and began to read in an effort to build back up my spirits and hope. While reading, I came across 2 Kings 6:6 and my spirit man leaped as my faith came alive. I said to myself, "If Elisha by faith could defy natural laws and cause the axe head to float, then I can use my faith to get my car back." The next five days during my work lunch break, I would go back to my place of employment, sit on a bench, pray, and declare, "God you are releasing the 'floating axe head' anointing into my situation that will overcome the company's policy."

I stirred myself up to call one more time releasing my faith that had been built up from meditating upon and confessing the Word of God. This time, the company went against its on policy and agreed to return the vehicle to me if I fulfilled certain payment arrangements. Good friends of mine drove me to the auto auction which was three hours away and I praised God as I was able to recover my vehicle. Man has policies, but God has a policy to back those that believe in Him.

MAN'S LAW VS GOD'S LAW

While we were engaged, my now wife went to visit her friends in central Virginia. God had been moving greatly at the church that we had been attending. Although she was out of town, she didn't want to miss what God would do in Sunday service. She decided to wake up early and complete the three-hour drive from out of town back to Virginia Beach. Her excitement to arrive at the place of worship must have led to her driving 80 mph. Unfortunately, the police officer who pulled her over was not as excited about her speeding to go to church. He gave her a traffic citation for reckless driving for being 15 mph over the speed limit. She arrived at church on time but what was once excitement was now soured by the violation that would go on her record and the accompanying hefty fine.

Two weeks later, official paperwork arrived from the court within the county that my wife had violated the speeding law. This county was known to be tough on traffic violations. The fine was $1200 to be on or before the scheduled court date and then an additional $500 fine per year for the next three years. We felt that the amounts were exorbitant. Also, it was unusual to have to pay a traffic fine for subsequent years after the violation. My wife didn't have a source of regular income as she was enrolled in college pursuing her master's degree. Additionally, I was having my own monetary problems and sadly unable to offer any financial assistance. In slang terms, we were broke as a bag of glass! Our wedding was the next year and we had struggled to save up money to pay for it. These extra expenses presented a great burden for us. We were also faced with the possibility that if the fine was not paid my fiancée (now wife) could face jail time.

We met at my home and prayed the prayer of agreement. Jesus said in Matthew 18:19 KJV, "Again I say unto you, that if two of you shall agree on earth as touching anything that they shall ask, it shall be done for them by my father which is in heaven." In prayer, we turned the issue over to God and asked that either He supply the money to pay the fine or help us resolve it by some other means. As the court date approached, the hefty fine loomed over my wife's head. We reminded God that He was our source and that the reason she was speeding was to attend Sunday morning worship service. We prayed, gave thanks, and left the ball in God's court.

A few weeks later, another envelope arrived from the court's office. My wife hesitantly opened it and began to read it. It was good news! Very good news! The county sent out letters to several people dismissing their fines and court dates. The Supreme Court of Virginia instituted a uniform fine schedule for traffic infractions that overruled local county ordinances. When my wife shared the good news with me, we both smiled, blessed God, and let out a big HALLELUJAH! In our opinion, God changed the laws just for us in response to our prayers. In this situation, God's law of the power of agreement (Matthew 18:19, 2 Corinthians 13:1, Deuteronomy 19:15) prevailed over the laws of man.

Daniel's enemies wanted to derail his political career and destroy his influence with the King of Persia. Daniel 6:5 says, "Then said these men, we shall not find any occasion against Daniel, except we find it against him in the law of his God." They connived together to institute laws contrary to the Mosaic laws of God that would entrap Daniel. Daniel 6:8 says, "Now, O King, establish the decree, and sign the writing, that it be not changed, according to the law of the Medes and Persians which change not." Judicial laws in themselves are difficult to challenge but the Persians governmental system was even stricter as a decree by its rulers could not be changed or revoked. Even the King of Persia himself didn't possess the authority to alter a decree or legislative order. A law had been passed that anyone who petitioned anyone except the king for 30 days would be thrown into the lion's den. Daniel was thrown into the lion's den as capital punishment for praying to God.

Daniel was cast into the den of carnivorous lions with the expectation of all that he would be devoured. In the morning time, he was found unharmed by the lions. Daniel 6:22 says, "My God has sent his angel and shut the lions' mouth that they have not hurt me." A law of man meant to bring death failed when God's miraculous saving power intervened. Daniel 6:23 says, "...no manner of hurt was found upon him because he believed in his God." Jesus taught in Mark 9:23, "All things are possible to them that believe." Those same individuals who meant Daniel harm then became subjected to new laws passed by the king. Daniel 6:24 reveals, "And the king commanded,

and they brought those men which had accused
Daniel, and they cast them into the den of lions,
them, their children, and their wives; and the lions had the mastery of them, and brake all their
bones in pieces or ever they came at the bottom
of the den."

DUAL-CITIZENSHIP

We must understand as believers in Jesus
Christ that we have dual-citizenship. When we
repented of our sins, confessed Jesus Christ as
Savior, and received Him as our Lord, we were
instantly engrafted into the Kingdom of God.
Because this process is invisible and automatic,
many are ignorant of the benefits of their heavenly citizenship. As believers, we are of the earth
but born of the Spirit. You may live in the United
States of America, Nigeria, Brazil, France or
some other nation and be a citizen within your
respective nation.

There exist laws, statues, and ordinances that
apply within each kingdom and nation. The same
applies for the Kingdom of God. Diverse laws
such as the law of faith, the law of obedience, the

law of the command, the law of the Spirit of life in Christ Jesus, and many other such laws apply to the life of the believer. When we are ignorant of these laws or negligent to apply them within our lives, then we lose the life, favor, and power they are meant to produce. Because the Kingdom of God is the primordial Kingdom that all other kingdoms, nations, tribes, and life originated from, it is superior to them all.

Hebrews 12:28 states, "Wherefore we receiving a kingdom which cannot be moved, let us have grace, whereby we may serve God acceptably with reverence and godly fear." Great and mighty empires have dominated their age and eras. The empires of Rome, Persia, Babylon, China, Egypt, and Great Britain were all shaken and diminished in influence and power. God's empire has not and cannot be shaken by the tides of time and the affairs of men.

In earthly affairs, one kingdom or nation dominates or conquers another often through physical force, war, and military might. The Kingdom of God in this current dispensation does not use war or physical power to conquer an earthly kingdom.

It does however cause its laws and ordinances to override the laws of man, laws of physical science, and laws of physics when needed. This is one of the reasons there was great confusion about the nature of Jesus' kingship and Kingdom during His ministry within the earth. Many of the disciples were expecting a Messiah who would appear in the land of Israel and lead a violent rebellion to overthrow the occupying Roman forces. Past heroes in Hebraic history such as King David, the Maccabee brothers, Samson, and Gideon had brought victory to Israel through physical warfare. Many were expecting the promised Messiah to do the same. Instead, Jesus taught them in Luke 17:21, "For behold, the Kingdom of God is within you!"

When a person applies for citizenship, they receive naturalization papers certifying their newly acquired citizenship. In the Kingdom of God, there are no physical papers to prove our citizenship; instead, the laws, judgments, and love of God must be imprinted within our mind and soul. The Kingdom of God is truly within. Within is where we will draw out God's miracle-working power to exercise the laws of God that supersede the laws of man! See the Kingdom within you!

Because we have spent our entire life learning, developing, and listening to the ways of man, it is often difficult to enter into the ways of God. Isaiah 55:8-9 say, "for my thoughts are not your thoughts, neither are your ways my way, declares the Lord. Even as the heavens are higher than the earth, so are my ways higher than your ways and my thoughts higher than your thoughts." Although the passage says God's ways and thoughts are unlike ours, it does not say that we are unable to obtain His ways and thoughts. Please note that God was speaking to a backslidden Israel through the prophet Isaiah. Having traveled to many nations around the world, I have personally experienced how culture affects people's attitudes, behaviors, belief systems, and religious practices.

We should be transformed by the culture of Heaven, but often we are conformed to the ways of the world. Romans 12:12 KJV says "Be not conformed to this world." The New Living Translation says, "Don't copy the behavior and customs of this world, but let God transform you..." Cultural assimilation is the process in which a minority culture or people group comes to mirror the actions, mindsets, and behaviors of a dominant group.

The Kingdom of Heaven is the dominant and noblest culture in all creation. There must be a seasoned resistance and immersion within the life of the believer where we are less connected from earthly culture and more acclimated to the culture of heaven. A new identity in Christ is found when we slightly withdraw from our own culture to explore and identify with the culture of Heaven. One cannot expect to experience supernatural miracles while still operating in the cultural mindset of the world age. As your thoughts rise to the level of the thoughts of God, your ways will follow and then you will begin to operate in miracles that defy man's written laws.

Create Your Miracle Circle

INPUTS AND OUTPUTS

"No man is an island" was a phrase made popular by English poet John Donne in his poetic work Devotions Upon Emergent Occasions in 1624. For hundreds of years, this saying has rung true in the hearts of men, women, and communities. This statement supports the argument that individuals and communities fail to thrive when isolated but grow when connected to other individuals and communities. The same can be said of the believer who desires to walk in miracle-receiving faith. It is important to create and monitor what I would like to call your "miracle circle!"

Our brains and souls operate as a kind of living computer memory bank. Many of our actions and behaviors are fueled by the memories, experiences, lessons, and environments that we have been exposed to at an early age. Daily, we are receiving data input from the world around us. Imagery and commentary frequently is being downloaded to our inner man from our family, friends, co-workers, television, radio, the internet, and many other sources. These are called inputs. They affect the outputs that we experience. Outputs are moods, actions, behaviors, motivations, emotional states, etc. We may desire to experience God's supernatural presence and power, but we are too reckless with allowing the wrong inputs into our brain and soul. These wrong inputs affect our mind, will, and emotions in a way that can rob us of our faith.

While it is humanly impossible to escape every negative input, it is not impossible to create a miracle circle for yourself. A miracle circle is being intentional about who and what has access to your ear and eye gates. There exist gates to the soul and the ears, and our eyes are the two primary modes of information reaching our soul. 1 John 2:16 tells us, "for all that is in the world is the lust of the flesh, the lust of the eyes, and the pride of life, is not of the Father, but of the world!" When the world system dominates and influences one's actions, then one becomes worldly! When the Word of God dominates and influences your actions, then you become spiritual!

There is no way around it, miracles require faith! Often times, we are a recipient of a miracle that is a sovereign act of God's mercy. Although these divine acts are powerful and needed, we cannot always depend upon them. When we learn the principles of God's Word and Kingdom, then we can expect our lives to become supernaturally charged. Guarding your ears, eyes, soul, and brain is in effect guarding your faith. Jesus posed the question to His disciples in Luke 18:8, "When the Son of Man comes will he find faith on the earth?" Please note that He didn't say, 'will He find prayer, singing, dancing, or festivals?" He specifically referred to faith. Prayer is important, but prayer not backed by faith is often empty words. Everything we do in our Kingdom walk must contain faith to be pleasing to God. Hebrews 11:6 says, "Without faith it is impossible to please God!"

GUARDING YOUR MIRACLE CIRCLE

One of the biggest influences upon our faith is people. That person who has access to our time, space, and energy is very vital. The right people help us to receive the right results. When creating your miracle circle, take note of those who have positive energy, are encouraging, and speak words filled with faith. They will help to water the seeds of the Word in your heart. The wrong people speaking into your ears will cause seeds of doubt, unbelief, and uncertainty to be sown. When this happens, we often become double-minded and hesitant about moving upon the things that God has spoken for us to do. When both seeds of faith and unbelief grow at the same time, then we become unstable. Instability in our desires, focus, and faith produces an aborted harvest. James 1:8 says, "A double minded man is unstable in all of his ways!"

Often times, the individuals closest to us are our family members. They know us better than anyone else and also are aware of our shortcomings, limitations, and inhibitions. Fortunately, the Spirit of God can surprise your family with blessing and using you in ways they never imagined. Because of the intimate proximity that family members enjoy, we have to be cautious not to allow them to hinder our faith and the miracle process. The times that we really need to hear God the most is often when we must make a major life decision or under tremendous pressure that requires a supernatural breakthrough.

You may find yourself full of faith until you call one relative who totally deflates your faith and fills your heart with doubt by questioning if you are being led by God. Many of Jesus' own relatives did not believe on Him or the legitimacy of His ministry. John 7:5 says, "For even his own brothers did not believe on him."

Friends and family may present an obstacle to our faith and our effort in walking out the miracle-receiving process. While we don't want to disconnect from them, often times God may require us to distance ourselves temporarily in order to better hear His voice. Jesus would constantly retreat to the mountains or a solitary place to pray. Mark 1:35 says, "And in the morning, rising up a great while before day, he went out and departed into a solitary place, and prayed."

Jesus would leave His family and surroundings where His faith and spiritual ears might be influenced by things in the natural to a place uncontaminated with fear, doubt, and unbelief. How many times have you tried to pray and someone or something intercepted you within your own house? When expecting a miracle from God, the miracle circle becomes useful because it helps you to set boundaries to keep faith-building people and things within your circle and lessen negative influences.

Many of us have home security systems that alert us when there is an intruder or unauthorized access of our doors and windows. We are taught to guard our property, families, and belongings but not taught to guard our inner man. Many of the internal conflicts, emotional instabilities, and insecurities people experience are due to an unguarded heart.

Proverbs 4:23 says, "Above all else, guard your heart for out of it flows the issues of life." The issues of life flow from the inside out. The Bible metaphorically uses flowing waters to symbolize how the condition of our inner man correlates to the condition of our lives. A murky contaminated heart will often lead to a defeated and depressed life. A peaceful and joyful life is a by-product of a clean and pure heart. We can train our spirit man to be alert to shut off our ears and soul to any pessimistic thoughts or conversations. Activate your internal security system by being full of the Word of God.

GET PLUGGED IN

There are many believers who have suffered in silence unnecessarily because they are disconnected from the Body of Christ. It is important to be plugged into the right believers and leader-ship. There has been an overemphasis on church membership and an under-emphasis on right relationships within the Kingdom of God. Hebrews 10:25 states, "not forsaking the assembling of ourselves together, as a manner of some is: but exhorting one another." When we gather together with other believers, it should be with faith-filled believers who can help sharpen us and build our faith. To exhort means to encourage. We all are constantly in need of encouragement.

Years ago, a couple named Richard and Jackie invited me out to dinner at a local steakhouse. When I went to the restroom, I heard God speak to me clearly, "Spend some time with these people!" That dinner was the start of a long-term relationship. We began to frequently pray and worship together often for hours at a time. God would give them dreams, visions, and prophetic words for my life. These revelations would often come at crucial times during the season of life where I had many challenges. My faith grew greatly, and I was encouraged by it and other divine relationships to grab hold of God's miracle promises for my life.

There are many gifts or offices (Ephesians 4:11) that God uses to help aid in the supernatural healing, deliverance, miracle, and breakthrough process. Throughout the Bible, especially in the Old Testament, prophets were used as vessels to help individuals receive miracles. 2 Kings 4:1 says, "Now there cried a certain woman of the wives of the sons of the prophet" and Exodus 3:9 says, "Now therefore behold the cry of the children of Israel is come unto me." In both verses, God responds to the cry of His people for help.

When we cry out to God for a miracle or breakthrough, He may raise up one of His servants with a greater anointing and faith than we possess to act as an intervening agent on our behalf. Elisha and the widow's oil being multiplied (2 Kings 4:1-7), the resurrection of the widow's son through Elijah (1 Kings 17:22), and Moses parting the Red Sea (Exodus 14:21) are all examples of prophets being sent as part of God's intervention system.

I grew up in a very traditional church where I learned the basics of the Bible. The pastor preached about salvation, communion, baptism, church membership, and many other fundamental tenets of the Bible. The church did not teach the full counsel of God (Acts 20:27), but a foundation was laid for my Christian life. Many years later, God led me to join a Spirit-filled ministry where the pastor taught us how to walk in faith, stand on the Word of God, and see God move in miracle-working power. There are over a hundred churches in my region, but God chose that one specific ministry for me to learn and grow. Week in and week out, I heard faith-building and the unadulterated Word of God preached from the pulpit. Romans 10:17 says, "Faith comes by hearing, and hearing by the Word of God."

Many are planted in churches that God never intended for them to join. Some of these ministries water down the Word, introduce concepts that steal faith, and don't believe that miracles are for today. Sitting under a ministry that doesn't believe the same Jesus who worked miracles yesterday can do the same today in the life of everyday people can be detrimental. Hebrews

13:8 affirms, "Jesus the same yesterday, today, and forever!"

Repentance Clears the Path

DON'T DESPISE THE SIMPLISTIC

Many regard the supernatural and the miraculous as fanatical, mystical, and spooky. One may expect principles that unlock miracles and breakthrough to be complex or grievous. A forty-day water-only fast, climbing a mountain and living in a cave alone with God for many days, and shedding mourning tears before God for hours are some of the principles that I have been taught in the past. These methods do have their validity and purpose but are often too extreme for the average believer. Work schedules, parental duties, and the responsibilities of life often make it too difficult to follow some of the extreme actions believers in ancient times and third world countries have taken to receive miracle breakthrough. More simplistic principles are often overlooked or devalued. One of those principles is repentance.

There is great power in repentance. I have heard repentance taught in a way that relegates its power to the believer's initial salvation experience and confession of major sins such as adultery, murder, or robbery. Repentance is not just for salvation and obvious sins, but also for hidden faults, unbiblical actions, and bad decisions that we make. Merriam-Webster's dictionary defines the word repent as, "to turn from sin and dedicate oneself to the amendments of one's life, to feel regret or contrition, or to change one's mind." In the Bible, when someone repented, they not only felt sorrow for their actions, but they also changed their actions. Repentance is the power of the Holy Spirit at work to bring inner change in the life and the heart open to His conviction.

THE PERFECT STORM

When you hear the word repent, what comes to mind? Sin and wrongdoing are probably your two answers, but repentance plays a powerful role in the miracle-working process as well. A life experience taught me this lesson even before I discovered this truth within the Bible. In eighth-grade, our English class was assigned a project to create a short story non-fiction work or book of poems for the Young Author's program. Each student had to create their own content, book cover, illustrations, and book binding. The teacher gave us a deadline that allowed four months for completion.

Four months should have been ample time for me to finish the project, but an enemy named procrastination got the best of me. I waited two days before the due date to start! I had to run around town to purchase the proper paper, book cover, glue, tape, colored pencils, and binding material needed for the physical book. Worst yet,

I had to write an entire short story in less than 2 days. I didn't own a computer or word processor but a typewriter. Anyone that has ever used an old typewriter knows that if you make a mistake or too many corrections, the document must be started again. The night before the due date, my mother fussed at me for waiting to the last days to start. She gave me a double rebuke for breaking her sleep with the loud sounds of the typewriter in action, typing 50 words per minute at 3:00 am.

I looked up at the clock and it was approaching 4:00 am. My eyes were red and burning from being up late at night. My hands were tired from banging away the typewriter. My mind was racing because if my project was unfinished, my teacher would be unforgiving. She had warned us multiple times that late work would not be accepted. The book submission accounted for 25% of our grade for the year. That meant if the project was not turned in, then the best grade I could receive out of the class would be a C- or D+. I was too burnt out to keep going.

If I quit now and lay down, at least I would get a few hours of sleep before what was guaranteed to be a sulky day at school the next morning. Before I went to bed, I prayed and repented. I felt bad for wasting time and now being in-between the proverbial rock and a hard place. "God, I need your help. I messed up. There is no reason that I should have waited to the last minute to work on this project. Please have mercy on me. Please let the teacher accept my work late. I accept total blame but please help me." I prayed the prayer of repentance while asking for mercy.

When you are under pressure, your nights are never long enough. I awoke with a sense of dismay. As I was getting dressed for school, my mother yelled out to me, "What are you getting dressed for? There is no school today!" I said, "Yes, there is school today. It is Friday!" She then told me that it snowed so heavy overnight that school had been canceled until Monday. I quickly peaked outside of my bedroom window and to my disbelief, the ground was covered in snow. School was cancelled due to the snow which gave me a three-day weekend to complete my work. God had answered my prayer!

You may be thinking, "What is the big deal about snow?" Well, you must understand firstly there had been no forecast of snow. When I watched the news, the meteorologist and news reporters were baffled by the snowfall. In addition, it was the first week in April. It never snows in my home state in the month of April. The previous days had just been warm weather. Deep within, I knew that God had accepted my words of repentance and plea for mercy! Yes, Jesus caused a miracle snow fall just for me!

CULTURE FOR THE MIRACULOUS

One of the earmarks of the Early Church and the Book of Acts are the notable miracles that took place. The blind seeing, lame walking, prison doors supernaturally opening up, and people getting raised from the dead were common place in early Christianity. I believe they experienced a culture of miracles because they lived in a culture of repentance. Peter's initial sermon concluded with an exhortation for repentance (Acts 2:38). The Holy Spirit maintained this atmosphere of holiness and repentance by bringing judgment on the unrepentant Ananias and Sapphira (Acts 5:1-11). Jeremiah 5:25 says, "Your sins have withheld good things from you." When we repent, we remove barriers that could be holding back blessings, healings, favor, and miracles from us.

John 5:5 says, "And a certain man was there, which had infirmity thirty and eight years." It is obvious that this man was crippled because Jesus told Him in verse 8, "Rise, take up thy bed, and walk." The lame was made to walk through the miracle power of Jesus Christ. John 5:14 then adds, "Afterward Jesus findeth him in the temple, and said unto him, Behold thou art made whole: sin no more, lest a worse thing come unto thee." It is evident that Jesus knew the root causes of the man's infirmity and the verse indirectly implies that it was caused by some sinful action. In this passage, we discover the miracle in connection to repentance. God can release miracles, but He has a prerequisite that we have a repentant heart.

"YOU GOT MAIL!"

After receiving a bachelor's degree with a double major from Old Dominion University, my wife decided to pursue a post-graduate degree. She applied to a local university with the hopes of acceptance. Two months before the semester was to start, she realized that the school hadn't approved her application and she had not completed her GREs. The GREs or Graduate Record Examinations is a test that is an admissions requirement for many graduate schools within the USA. The test measures graduate school candidates' skill level in reasoning and analytical writing. There is a nominal fee for the exam and for the material to practice for it.

My wife called me and asked what she should do. I told her we must agree in prayer for a miracle. Matthew 18:19 says, "Again I say unto you, that if two of you shall agree on earth as touching anything that they ask, it shall be done for them by My Father in heaven." My wife started the prayer with asking God to forgive her for missing the deadline to take the GREs. We asked God to work it out so that she would be able to attend school that semester. Literally, ten minutes after we hung up the phone, an email arrived in my wife's inbox from the university. She opened and to her surprise, it was someone from the admission's office saying that my wife was eligible for a GRE waiver! The only requirement was for her to fill out a short form and complete a short essay! Until this day, we have no idea how the person knew that my wife had not completed her GRE. We rejoiced over this miracle email!

The Master of Miracles

THE PRINCIPAL PERSON

There are many spiritual principles and variables involved in the production of the miraculous. Many of them have already been mentioned in this book including faith, allowing God to decide the method of the miracle, prayer, being at the right place at the right time, etc. While this book mainly covers principles and wisdom keys to receiving the supernatural from God, this chapter will address "The Master of Miracles." The Master of Miracles isn't a principle but He is the principal person that breathes life into every principle of the Kingdom of God.

Throughout the Bible, we read about great men and women used by God do extraordinary feats. We've all read about some of the fantastic events that we encounter in the Word of God including Elijah calling down fire, Moses dividing the Red Sea, Joshua stopping the Sun from moving, and Samson's mighty feats of strength. These figures' names have been remembered in history for being vessels for the supernatural. Although they all demonstrated their own greatness, there is only one "Master of Miracles." The Holy Spirit has been involved in every miracle past and present.

One cannot expect to walk in God's supernatural power without a relationship with the Holy Spirit. He is the active force that works behind the scenes to bring forth miracles, healing, deliverance, unusual financial blessings, and breakthroughs. I must issue a disclaimer. Desiring the supernatural, spirit realm, or miracles without a proper relationship with the Holy Spirit can be dangerous. Many have opened themselves up to ungodly and familiar spirits by trying to "tap into" the things of the spirit realm outside of the guidance of the Holy Spirit. The Kingdom of God is accessible to those who have been born again, received Jesus Christ as their Savior, and received the Spirit of God within their hearts. 2 Corinthians 1:22 says, "Who has sealed us and given the earnest of the Spirit in our hearts."

CO-LABORERS WITH THE SPIRIT

God has called us to be co-laborers and joint-heirs (Romans 8:17) with Him through Christ Jesus. As we grow in the supernatural, we should also be growing in our ability to work with the Holy Spirit. When we pray, God often responds first not by sending the answer to prayer but by releasing the Holy Spirit to give us wisdom, in-struction, or insight that is needed. Oftentimes, we overlook the instructions from the Holy Spirit but complain that God is not answer-ing our prayers. In the Bible, we find that when God wanted to perform an extraordinary act, He would often first move upon a man or woman by His Spirit. This is where we read that "the hand of the Lord" (2 Kings 3:15, Ezekiel 37:1) or the Spirit of God came upon a person (Judges 14:6, Judges 3:10, 1 Samuel 16:13) as a precursor to a mighty act.

Jesus' ministry was filled with many supernatural feats such as the blind seeing, lame healed, deaf hearing, walking on water, casting out demons, and turning water into wine. The secret of His ministry's power was His being surrendered to the Holy's Spirit in His life. We have no record of Jesus doing any miracles before the Holy Spirit descended upon His life. Matthew 3:16 says, "And Jesus when he was baptized, went straightway out of the water; and lo the heavens were opened unto him, and he saw the Spirit of God descending like a dove, and lighting upon him."

Jesus in His own words shares with us the source of His ability to free spiritual prisoners, open blind eyes, and heal the brokenhearted in Luke 4:18, "The Spirit of the Lord is upon me, because he has anointed me to preach the gospel to the poor; he has sent me to heal the brokenhearted, to preach deliverance to the captives, and recovering of sight to the blind, to set at liberty them that are bruised." Every miracle Jesus did, the Holy Spirit was directly involved.

My own ministry has been filled with many notable miracles. Frequently, we have received testimonies of lives changed by the power of God. I have personally seen the lame walk, people discard walkers, canes, or crutches, the deaf ears opened, cancers destroyed, and as many as 10 partially or fully blind see in one meeting! We always have credited these extraordinary happenings to the love of God and the working of the Holy Spirit. While many pray for the power of the Holy Spirit, few learn to yield to His presence and power. One will recognize His presence almost instantly by spending consistent quality time in the Word, worship, and prayer.

A MIGHTY PRAYER WEAPON

Jesus was always teaching and equipping His disciples to live the Kingdom of God lifestyles and for the work of ministry. He shared many revelations and truths with them, but it was not until after His ascension that a new spiritual weapon was released to them. Acts 2:4 says, "And they were filled with the Holy Ghost, and began to speak with other tongues, as the Spirit gave them utterance." The Apostles received a spiritual prayer language whereby they could communicate with God spirit to spirit. One of the reasons the Early Church constantly saw the power of God at work was because they valued praying in tongues. The Apostle Paul said in 1 Corinthians 14:18, "I thank God that I speak in tongues more than you all."

Jude 1:20 states, "But ye, beloved, building up yourselves on your most holy faith, praying in the Holy Ghost." Praying in tongues stirs up our faith and builds us up to receive from God. Once before a meeting, God had me to pray in tongues for one hour. During the meeting, I went to the altar to receive prayer but when the altar workers touched me, they felt the fire of God coming off of my person. The main altar worker looked at me startled. He said, "You don't need to be in the line for prayer. You need to be the one praying for people." Quickly he positioned me at the altar to pray for souls who were hungry for God. I

attributed this Holy Spirit fire that brought healing and deliverance to the time God had me praying in tongues before the start of the meeting.

Some believe that tongues are useless. They
argue that it's purposeless to pray in tongues if
one is unable to understand what is being said.
My response is found in 1 Corinthians 14:2, "For
he that speaks in an unknown tongues speaks not
unto men, but unto God; for no man understan-
deth him; howbeit in the spirit he speaketh mysteries." Even the wisest person cannot foresee the
vicissitudes of life, but the Holy Spirit knows all.
When we pray in tongues, our spirit man engages
with the Spirit of God to pray about circumstances and things beyond our natural understanding.
When answers to prayers seem held up, praying
in tongues can demolish those unknown barriers
to our breakthrough.

I recall the story of a couple who was attempt-
ing to sell their home. Frustration set in when
they had their home on the market for several
months and there was no success with the home
sale. They tried lowering the home's sale price as
their tactics to attract a home buyer, but to no

avail. One day, while driving around town, they prayed together to God, "Dear Lord, we have tried everything to sell our home. We have even prayed and prayed but nothing has worked." The wife heard the voice of the Holy Spirit say, "But you have not prayed in tongues!" With nothing to lose, they pulled over on the side of the road and, with hand in hand, prayed fifteen minutes in tongues. Literally, half an hour later, they received a phone call from their realtor that a buyer was interested in their home. Praying in tongues released their breakthrough.

WHAT GOD TAUGHT ME!

Have you ever struggled to hear God's voice? We all have had that problem at some point in our spiritual walk. There have been times that I fasted and prayed desiring to hear God's voice concerning serious matters. One day, the Lord spoke to me, "Don't wait until you have a grave issue to try to hear from me. Learn to hear from me in the small affairs of life." After I began to follow God's instruction, hearing His voice no longer was a difficulty for me. In meetings, God often speaks to me unusual things to do or say that produce miracles. People are often astounded by these prophetic actions and even more by the supernatural results. Proverbs 3:6 says, "In all thy ways acknowledge him and he shall direct thy paths."

Five Things to Remember About the Holy Spirit

1. He is the "Miracle Maker" and invisibly works to produce breakthroughs on our behalf.

2. He is concerned about the small as well as major areas of your life.

3. You can speak to Him directly.

4. When His presence comes upon you, it energizes you to do the supernatural.

5. Hearing His voice is key to receiving instructions that help to release the miraculous.

Give God Something to Work With

JESUS' FIRST MIRACLE SECRET

When miracles manifest, they bring with them a sense of awe, wonder, and excitement. Some miracles are described as unexplainable. The effect of a miracle may be witnesses without the beholder understanding the causative factors of that miracle. Many pray for miracles to happen while neglecting to understand that we have to give God something to work with for the miracle to happen.

One can imagine God as a master builder who is able to produce great architectural works, but like any construction project, raw materials are needed to build. The same principle applies to us regarding the phenomena of miracles. The importance of this principle is evidenced by Jesus' first recorded miracle. At a wedding at Cana of Galilee, Jesus' mother Mary reports to Him that there is no more wine for the celebration.

John 2:6-9 says, "And there were set there six waterpots of stone, after the manner of the purifying of the Jews, containing two or three firkins apiece. Jesus saith unto them, Fill the waterpots with water. And they filled them up to the brim. And he saith unto them, Draw out now, and bear unto the governor of the feast. And they bare it. When the ruler of the feast had tasted the water that was made wine, and knew not whence it was."

Let's examine the methodology that Jesus used to supernaturally supply wine. Please note that He could have simply touched the water pot, wiggled His fingers a bit, and proclaimed "water now!" Instead He told them to fill the water pots with water. Jesus understood you cannot get something from nothing. The water was the instrument that God would use to produce wine, and the Holy Spirit's presence was the transforming factor. Notice that Jesus told them, "Fill it to the brim!" The more water inside of the water pots would equate to more wine produced. Even God Himself, when He desired to make man, He took him from the clay of the earth. Genesis 2:7 says, "Then the Lord God formed man from the dust of the ground."

FINANCIAL MIRACLES

Financial miracles are often the result of a financial seed sown in faith and in sacrifice. There is a saying, "Every seed produces after its own kind." Genesis 1:11 states there are "fruit tree yielding fruit after its kind." Almost every financial breakthrough that I experienced first involved me giving to someone else or another ministry first. I believe one of the reasons that the rich get richer is that many have mastered the principle of giving. Many well-known wealthy figures, such as Oprah and Bill Gates, give away multi-million dollars to charitable and worthy causes. Galatians 6:7, "Be not deceived, God is not mocked; for whatsoever a man soweth, that shall he also reap."

Many desire financial bliss but hold up their own blessing by being tight fist and stingy. I have seen several pray for million-dollar blessings but only give $100 offerings. 2 Corinthians 9:6 says, "But this I say, He which soweth sparingly shall reap also sparingly; and he which soweth bountifully shall reap also bountifully." God can multiply what we give Him, but we first have to give Him something to multiply. Just like Jesus' waterpots being filled to the brim, if we desire great financial harvest, we have to sow great financial seeds. Mark 4:24 says, "What measure ye mete; it shall be measured unto you."

One morning, I was reading the account of Jesus multiplying the fish and loaves. Our ministry had started to experience great healing and miracles, but I was always amazed by this miracle in Jesus' ministry. God spoke softly and with conviction to my heart, "Would you believe me for the same type of miracle?" That night in church, I decreed to our congregation that God was going to do a miracle of multiplication for us. I didn't imagine that the miracle would happen the exact same night. After service, two women who counted the money for the offering said as they counted the offering the second time, the amount increased. They counted a third time and again, the count increased significantly. Rarely were they inaccurate with the count and they remembered the decree that I made at the beginning of service. They counted it one more time and the same results! This was a miracle offering that God multiplied!

DIG A DITCH

The kings of Israel, Judah, and Edom were in alliance to fight against the king of Moab. It appeared that they would lose the battle and suffer an imminent defeat. The prophet Elisha was summoned to speak the word of the Lord that might turn the tide of affairs. 2 Kings 3:16 says,

"And he said, thus saith the Lord, make this valley full of ditches." Instead of prophesying some great military strategy, he simply ordered them to dig ditches. 2 Kings 3:17 then continues, "For thus says the Lord, ye shall not see wind, neither shall you see rain, yet this valley shall be filled with water." Through a series of events, God used the ditches and the reflection from the water that looked like blood when the sun shone upon it to gain a victory for His people. Dig God a ditch and watch Him fill it!

GIVE HIM SOMETHING TO FILL

Years ago, I was set to go to Regent University to hear a notable evangelist speak on campus. When I arrived at the school, there was a disappointing announcement that the evangelist had taken ill and would not be on site. In place of the evangelist, a missionary leader from the Chinese underground church would be speaking. This gentleman was in America to raise awareness and support for Chinese missionaries and pastors that needed resources and training. Due to the persecution from the Chinese government, a plan was set in place to train the emerging Chinese ministers outside of the nation in the Philippines. An old warehouse was acquired to house up to 30 ministers to be trained in evangelism, discipleship, and church leadership.

When the leaders of this project entered the facility, they realized some details had been neglected in the planning. In two weeks, over two dozen students would be showing up from China at the school, but they would have no beds to sleep. They prayed and prayed together asking God to send someone to buy beds for the ministry. The next day, when they returned to the facility to continue in prayer, mysteriously a dozen sets of bunk beds miraculously appeared. They were overcome with joy but also shocked with awe because there was no explanation to how these beds appeared. No one in the local region knew the purpose of the facility and they had not made their needs known to anyone but God.

God had supernaturally delivered beds to the facility, but there still were not enough desks, chairs, and tables for the soon arriving students.

The project leaders did what they knew to do best, PRAY! They prayed again to God asking for support for the work of ministry. The next day, they returned again to the facility to find that desks, tables, chairs, and even books were present. They were elated and even more encouraged for the work of the Lord. As they investigated what may have taken place to supply their needs, there was no sign of forced entry into the building. Also, it would take the effort of several men to bring in beds, chairs, desks, and tables. All of this would have to be done unnoticed by anyone. A true miracle indeed! They gave God something to work with by buying the warehouse facility and releasing their faith. God supernaturally furnished it for the work of the ministry.

A LAW OF PHYSICS

The Law of the Conservation of Mass, as stated by Albert Einstein, states, "Energy cannot be created or destroyed, it can only be changed from one form to another." This means that something cannot be made from nothing. It also means that mass, substance, energy, a chemical, or object of one form with the right forces affecting it can be changed into another form. When God commissioned Moses to be a deliverer, He asked him, "What do you have available that can be a vehicle for my miraculous power?" Exodus 4:2-3 says, "And the Lord said unto him, what is in thy hand? and he said a rod! And he said, Cast it on the ground. And he cast it on the ground, and it became a serpent; and Moses fled from before it." Like Moses, there is a miracle in your hand!

Commit the Miracle into His Hands

YOUR SEED MUST DIE

Every manifestation of a miracle results from a process that involves different spiritual elements such as faith, timing, waiting on God, sowing, and watering. One can think of producing a miracle in much the same way a cook would

bake a cake. The first step in baking a cake is se-
lecting your ingredients. Flour, eggs, salt, milk,
extracts, flavorings, and cooking oil are some of
the basic ingredients needed to bake a cake. It is
also equally important the ingredients be mea-
sured and mixed in the correct proportions. One
of the most challenging and difficult ingredients
to master in your miracle mix is turning your
miracle over to God.

One of the highest demonstrations of faith is
walking away from our miracle and turning it
completely over to God. After we have exercised
the principles discussed in this book, there comes
a time where the last step is to commit our breakthrough to God. Miracles are supernatural. But
what is the supernatural? An easy way to define
the supernatural is God's SUPER grace, favor,
mercy, and power on top of our NATURAL ef-
forts and faith. Simply put, it's God's super and
our natural combined to produce divine synergy—miracle. The Bible says in 1 Corinthians
15: 46 says, "Howbeit that was not first which
is spiritual, but that which is natural: and afterward that which is spiritual."

Using our natural man to apply the principles
of the Word of God is likened unto our effort in
combining the cake ingredients. Placing the miracle in the hands of God and out of ours is likened
to placing the miracle into a spiritual oven waiting for it to bake.

Earlier in this book, you were taught about
sowing a seed for your miracle, watering it with
the Word and faith, and then allowing God to
give the breakthrough. I would like to add that
God miraculously gives life to our seed through
the life-and-death process. Jesus often used language and concepts that the common people of
His day could comprehend. Many of His followers
were farmers and fishermen. He would use agrar-
ian principles to convey deep spiritual truths.

John 12:24 says, "Verily, verily I say unto you,
except a grain of wheat fall into the ground and
die, it abide alone; but if it die it bringeth forth
much fruit." The wheat farmer of His day would
have been familiar with the fact that the potential
in a wheat grain or any seed cannot be unlocked
until it falls to the ground. Although the fallen
seed becomes disconnected from the tree or plant

that was sustaining its life, when it falls into the ground, it can then produce a multiplied harvest. This is one of the "miracles" of nature.

The perfect example of this is found with God's best and most magnificent seed—His Son Jesus Christ. John 3:16 says, "For God so loved the world that he gave his only begotten Son, that whosoever shall believe on him shall not perish but have everlasting life." Note that God desired a harvest of spiritual sons and daughters who would inherit everlasting life, but He first had to give. God had to sow His only Son from heaven into the earth. The Spirit of God breathed life into the miracle seed named Jesus within the womb of a virgin mother named Mary. Wait; there is more to this story. Before the expected harvest of souls could be realized, the death had to come to the seed. Jesus had to commit Himself into the hands of God. Jesus had to die on the cross. The same seed that God breathed life into was required to die before potentially billions of souls could come to salvation.

CHANGE YOUR PERSPECTIVE

Prayer changes things. Prayer stirs up our faith. Prayer releases the power of God into the earth. Prayer breathes life to the Word of God in our hearts and is a necessary element for every miracle. Prayer is the vehicle by which we make our petitions and requests known unto God. Matthew 7:7 says, "Ask and it shall be given to you." There is also a saying, "You have not because you ask not!" If we follow the lives of holy men and women throughout the Bible and history, we find they were people of prayer. Many individuals that consistently experience the hand of God in their life and live under an open heaven pray, pray, and pray. I know from personal experience that prayer changes things and releases the dynamic power of God.

The praying man or woman most often is praying from the position of asking for God's aid or help. Although prayer is powerful and essential, there is a time that we need to change our spiritual perspective. There is a time to stop praying about a matter and switch to praising Him in advance for the answer to the prayer. Mark

11:24 says, "Whatsoever you desire, when you pray, believe that you receive them, and you shall have them." Jesus taught that after one prays, then there must be a mental adjustment to believing that one has already received the answer to prayer. We all have prayed with doubt that God has heard our prayers. We continue to pray faithless. When we have faith in God, our prayers are infused with confidence that He hears us! Once we have an inner witness that we have prayed in faith believing that we have received the answer in the spirit, even before the miracle manifests in the natural, then it's time to move from prayer to praise. Prayer says to God, 'I need your help.' Praise says, 'God, I'm thankful that you have already helped me!' Praise is one method of turning a situation over into the hands of God.

It is easy to give God thanksgiving and worship after money, a new job, healing, or a blessing happens in our life. We often desire to see our blessing before we can praise God for our blessing. The mature believer knows that 'seeing is believing,' but this person is not waiting to see with their natural eyes. Your eyes of faith must see the promises of God being delivered to you before you possess them in the natural. The end of prayer is praise, and the end of praise is worship. We move from the outer court to the inner courts of intimacy with Jesus as we transition into praise. As we are trusting God to see the miraculous in our life, He is also deepening our relationship with Him. The miracle may be important to us, but our growing in the knowledge of Christ is of primary importance to God.

In Acts 16, the Apostle Paul and Silas were beaten and thrown into prison for sharing their faith. The prisons of those days were much more horrendous than the austere conditions of modern-day, Westernized prison systems. They were thrown into the "inner prison" which was a dungeon and the worst part of the prison. Their feet were bound with metal shackles. Often prisoners would become ill from the poor sanitation, bacteria, and contagious infections from other diseased prisoners. In many of the cities, the inner prison was lower than the regular jail and thus the sewage system ran adjacent to it. The suffering was compounded by such awful smells that were toxic to inhale and could cause the toughest person to faint.

This Bible story happened in real life, but metaphorically represents the worse possible condition a human can be in, where all seems dark and hopeless. We find the solution to such travesty as we study the response of Paul and Silas. Acts 16: 25-26 says, "And at midnight Paul and Silas prayed, and sang praises unto God; and the prisoners heard them. And suddenly there was a great earthquake so that the foundations of the prison were shaken: and immediately all the doors were opened, and every one's bands were loosed." Praise, flowing out of "the depths of our heart releases suddenlies" where the answers to prayers have been held up.

JOY TURNS TO PAIN

My pastors many years ago had their first of two children—a beautiful baby girl named Amina. They had been married six years and decided to wait before having kids. The baby girl signaled a new season within their lives and marriage. They were elated to have their first child. Parents know the excitement and joy that a newborn baby adds to a household. Every smile, gesture, or new movement that a baby adds to their repertoire becomes entertainment for first time parents.

This family was overjoyed until one day baby Amina hit her head and it began to swell profusely. Baby Amina was crying uncontrollably and with discomfort. Both parents had served God in ministry and witnessed many miracles and instant healings. They began to pray for the swelling to go down, all to no avail. Both parents must have had an epiphany at the same time because their eyes simultaneously met conveying a sense of fear, grief and horror. They had prayed and there was nothing more they could do. The swelling and obvious damage to baby Amina's head would cost the young baby her life. The dad was a trained medical professional and doctor. He knew that even if an emergency response team arrived in an ambulance, it would be too late.

No parent should have to bury their child. Sadly, and with hesitation, they knew what needed to be done. Together they lifted baby Amina in the air and said, "God, you blessed us with this child and now we commit her back into your hands. Her life was for your glory!" They did not weep or curse God but uttered a prayer and simple act of thanksgiving. Suddenly, the young child stopped crying and her head began to return to normal size just as rapidly as it had swelled. They watched an instant miracle right before their eyes. They shouted and rejoiced together over the life-saving miracle that Jesus blessed them with. This is an example of how many times, at the end of our faith, we have to place our miracle in the hands of God. Today, Amina is happily married with three beautiful children of her own, and her testimony is part of a rich legacy of faith.

THE POWER OF PRAISE

Someone asked me once, "Demontae, how do I know when I'm finished praying?" I responded, "You will sense the victory in your heart and praise will swell up from the inside out." Pray until praise happens naturally and spontaneously. A good practice is to praise God before your miracle, in expectancy, and to praise God after your breakthrough shows up. Even once you receive an answer to prayer, the enemy may try to rob you. John 10:10 says, "The thief does not come except to steal, kill, and destroy." Elisha the servant of

God prophesied to the Shunammite woman (2 Kings 4:16-17), saying, "About this season, according to the time of life, thou shalt embrace a son.....and the woman conceived, and bare a son at that season that Elisha had said unto her, according to the time of life." We find later in this chapter that the same miracle child that this woman was blessed with suffered an injury while working in the field and died. The devil tried to steal back the miracle child by cutting his life off prematurely. Thankfully, God supernaturally raised the young man from the dead.

Here are five principles to remember about the power of praise as it relates to you seeing the supernatural hand of God in your life:

1. Praise tells God that you have received what you have asked for. It is an act of faith.

2. Praise switches your focus from self and your issues to God and His greatness.

3. Praise shows your appreciation for God's handiwork in your life.

4. Praise is the icing on the cake for your
    prayers. It helps to seal the prayers with
    thanksgiving.

5. Praise causes the prison doors in your life to
    blow wide open for you to walk out of them
    and receive your miracle.

About the Author

Demontae Edmonds is affectionately known as "The Miracle Man" due to the plethora of signs, wonders, and miracles that God has performed through his ministry. He is the former pastor of Freedom in Christ Church and founder of Freedom 4 the Nations. As an apostolic ministry leader, he has traveled the globe to over twenty nations declaring the Gospel of Jesus Christ. Throughout the United States, Europe, Asia, and Africa, he has seen the blind see, lame walk, deaf hear, the obese/overweight experience supernatural instant weight loss, limbs grow, and many other creative miracles.

As a highly sought-after prophetic voice, he has ministered to kings, CEOs, government officials, and church leaders. Pastors and leaders often gather at his meetings, and he has ministered to as many as 2500 church leaders in one ministry setting. Demontae has been the special guest on many regional, national, and international television and radio broadcast including TBN Praise the Lord, CBN International, Turning Point, UCB Radio, Atlanta Live, Premier Radio, Power Vision TV, Oracle Television, LATENA Radio, and Cable Africa Network. Many of his short articles have been published on The Elijah List and circulated to hundreds of thousands of readers. He is proudly married to his wife Jessica and they have three beautiful kids together.

Contact him online for your inquiries:
www.f4nations.com
www.youtube.com/ficmva
info@f4nations.com

Or write to:
Freedom 4 the Nations
P. O. Box 7294, Chesapeake, VA 23324

Appendix

Dr. Fred Price

7901 S. Vermont Avenue

Los Angeles, CA 90044

800.943.4388

http://www.faithdome.org

Index

A

ability, 1, 4, 12, 88–89
angel, 28, 31, 40, 60
announcement, 18
anointing, 74
answered prayers, 4
axe head, 51–53

B

barriers, 83
believers, 33, 62, 65, 67, 72, 78
blessing, 109
blood, 10, 100
borrow, 9

C

chronological time, 30
church, 57, 75

co-laborers, 88

communities, 66–67

conquers, 62

culture, 64–65, 82

D

damage, 5, 112

darkness, 47–48

depressed life, 72

Desperate times, 9

desperation, 9–10

dilemma, 52

Disappointment, 55

dispensation, 62

ditches, 100

divine judgment, 23

divine synergy, 105

doctors, 6, 32, 112

doors, 72, 111

dual-citizenship, 61

dual purposes, 51

E

earth, 2, 47, 63, 84, 108

embarrassment, 18
evangelist, 100
eyes, 80, 109, 112–13

F

faith, 1–5, 7–8, 12–13, 15, 46, 49, 52–54, 56, 67, 69–71, 73–74, 102, 105, 108–10, 113
fear, 23
feast, 96
Financial miracles, 17, 97

G

gates, 68
grab, 30–31, 73

H

harvest, 46, 107
healing, 98
healing waters, 29
heart, 7–8, 11–12, 16, 39–42, 49, 69–70, 72, 79, 108

I

income, 58

incurable disease, 23

incurable illness, 10

instructions, 88, 94

Isaiah, 18, 48–49, 64

J

Jesus, 7, 10, 33, 36, 68, 71, 82, 89, 96

joy, 101, 111

joyful life, 72

K

kairos, 30–31

kingdom, 27, 61

L

laws, 50, 53–54, 56, 59–60, 62–63, 65

life experience, 79

Location, 29

love, 13, 15, 46, 90

M

manifest, 22, 29, 34

master builder, 96

medical treatment, 10

mental adjustment, 109

mercy, 22, 68, 81

Messiah, 27, 63

metal screws, 4–5

metal shackles, 110

mindset, 52

ministry, 33, 36, 51, 63, 75, 90, 101–2, 112, 116

miracle, 1–2, 4–7, 13–15, 21–25, 29–33, 43–45, 47, 49, 53, 73–75, 81–83, 85–87, 93–97, 99, 101–13

miracle circle, 66, 68

miraculous, 4, 46, 86, 94

money, 20, 22, 40–42, 45–46, 58, 99

mortgage miracle, 21

Mosaic laws, 59

mundane, 30, 36

N

natural mind, 32

O

obstacle, 12, 71
oily, 22, 102

P

pessimistic thoughts, 72
phenomena, 29, 96
power, 34, 47, 54, 62, 78, 90–91, 108, 113–14
praise, 109–10, 114–15
prayers, 21, 31, 39–41, 58, 81, 88, 91, 108–9, 111, 113
principles, 2, 4, 6, 15, 40, 47, 53, 77–78, 86–87, 96, 98, 106, 114
promises, 18, 28, 32, 109
property, 27
prophet, 23–24, 33, 52, 74

R

relationship, 87, 110
repentance, 78, 81–83
repentant heart, 83
resources, 41, 100
restoration, 1

resurrection, 2

S

sacrificial, 44
season, 15, 28, 73, 111
seeds, 69
sleep, 80–81, 101
source, 57–58
sovereign act, 68
sower, 43
spiritual, 105
supernatural, 1, 43, 45–46, 77, 87, 94, 105
supernatural acts, 1, 52
supernatural debt cancellation, 9
supernatural flow, 37
supernatural miracles, 23, 42, 49
supernatural power, 87
surgery, 32

T

teacher, 79
testimonies, 13
tongues, 91–92
typewriter, 80

U

uncommon faith, 4, 6–7, 9–11
uncommon miracles, 9
unexpected miracle, 9
unguarded heart, 72
untraceable miracle, 21

V

victory, 100
voice, 6, 35, 41–42, 71, 93–94

W

water, 28–29, 47, 51, 53, 69, 89, 96–97, 100
windows, 31, 41, 72
worship, 16, 22, 34, 57, 73, 110

Lightning Source UK Ltd.
Milton Keynes UK
UKHW021126170519
342861UK00007B/647/P